Title: Brachiosaurus
R.L.: 4.1
PTS: 0.5
TST: 192960

Smithsonian

LITTLE EXPLORER

BRACHIOSAURUS

by Kathryn Clay

CAPSTONE PRESS
a capstone imprint

Little Explorer is published by Capstone Press,
1710 Roe Crest Drive, North Mankato, Minnesota 56003
www.mycapstone.com

The name of the Smithsonian Institution and the sunburst
logo are registered trademarks of the Smithsonian Institution.
For more information, please visit www.si.edu.

Library of Congress Cataloging-in-Publication Data
Library of Congress Cataloging-in-Publication Data
Names: Clay, Kathryn, author.
Title: Brachiosaurus / by Kathryn Clay.
Description: North Mankato, Minnesota : Capstone Press, [2018] |
Series: Smithsonian little explorer. Little paleontologist | Audience:
Age 5–9. | Audience: K to grade 3. | Includes bibliographical
references and index. Identifiers: LCCN 2017041320 (print) |
LCCN 2017047308 (ebook) | ISBN 9781543505504 (eBook PDF)
| ISBN 9781543505429 (library binding) | ISBN 9781543505467
(paperback) Subjects: LCSH: Brachiosaurus—Juvenile literature.
Classification: LCC QE862.S3 (ebook) | LCC QE862.S3 C53 2018
(print) | DDC 567.913—dc23
LC record available at https://lccn.loc.gov/2017041320

Editorial Credits
Michelle Hasselius, editor; Heidi Thompson, designer;
Eric Gohl, media researcher; Kathy McColley, production specialist

Our very special thanks to Matthew T. Miller, Paleontologist in
the Department of Paleobiology at the National Museum of Natural
History, Smithsonian Institution, for his review. Capstone would also
like to thank Kealy Gordon, Product Development Manager, and
the following at Smithsonian Enterprises: Ellen Nanney, Licensing
Manager; Brigid Ferraro, Vice President, Education and Consumer
Products; Carol LeBlanc, Senior Vice President, Education and
Consumer Products; and Christopher A. Liedel, President.

Image Credits
Alamy: Moviestore Collection Ltd, 28–29; Capstone: Jon Hughes,
cover, 2–3, 6–7, 12–13 (all), 16, 17, 18, 19, 23 (inset), 30–31; Getty
Images: Stocktrek Images/Corey Ford, 24, Tim Boyle, 25; iStockphoto:
MR1805, 10–11; Newscom: Photoshot/VW PICS/Sergi Rebordo,
27, Universal Images Group/De Agostini Picture Library, 9; Science
Source: Francois Gohier, 5 (inset), Julius T. Csotonyi, 4–5; Shutterstock:
Catmando, 20–21, 22–23, David Steele, 21 (inset), eva_mask, 1, Linda
Bucklin, 14–15, Luka Hercigonja, 19 (inset), Michael Rosskothen, 8,
Paul Banton, 7 (inset)

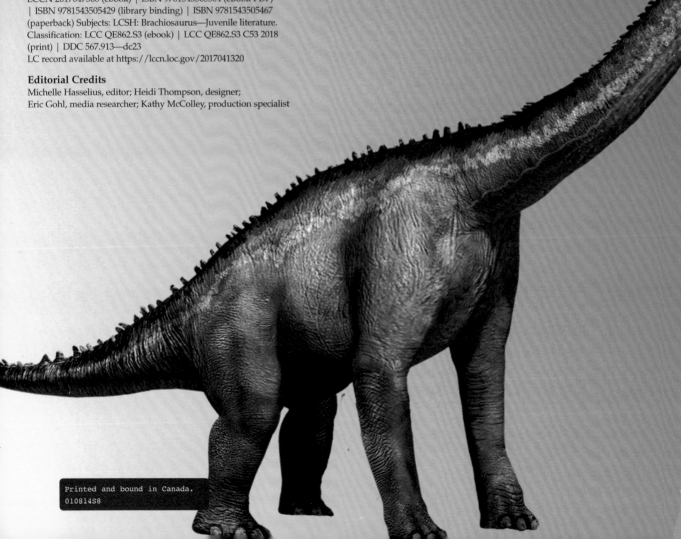

Printed and bound in Canada.
010814S8

TABLE OF CONTENTS

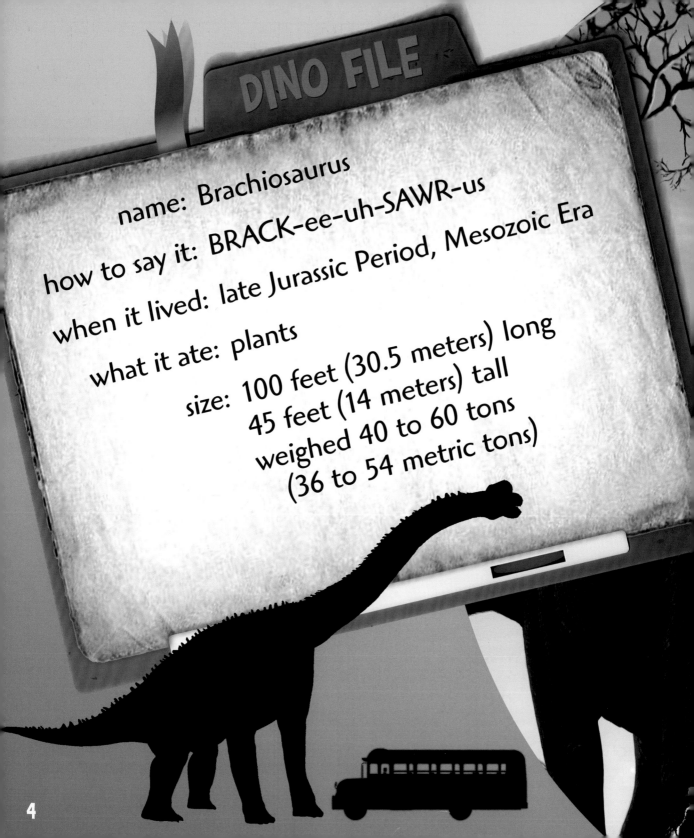

DINO FILE

name: Brachiosaurus

how to say it: BRACK-ee-uh-SAWR-us

when it lived: late Jurassic Period, Mesozoic Era

what it ate: plants

size: 100 feet (30.5 meters) long
45 feet (14 meters) tall
weighed 40 to 60 tons
(36 to 54 metric tons)

4

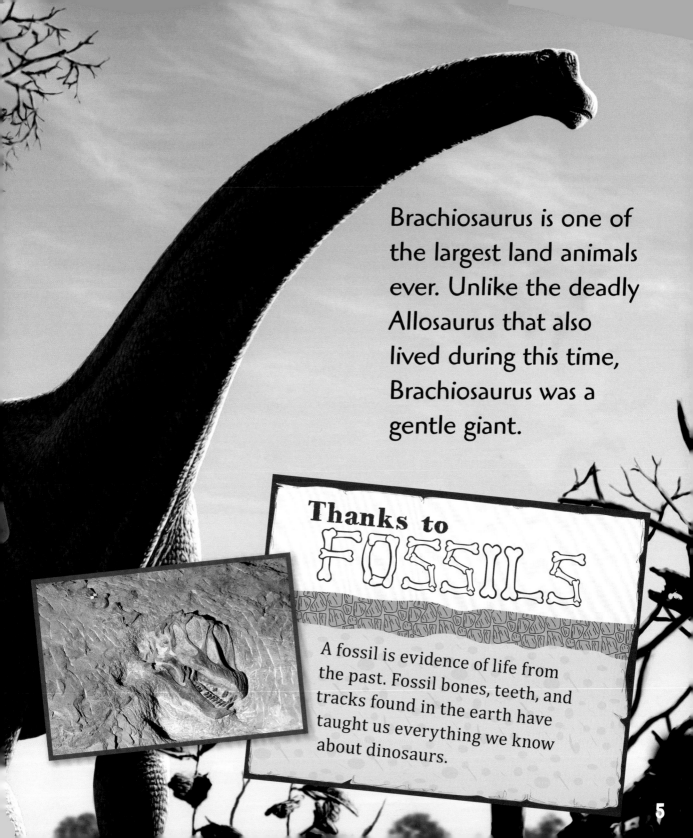

Brachiosaurus is one of the largest land animals ever. Unlike the deadly Allosaurus that also lived during this time, Brachiosaurus was a gentle giant.

Thanks to FOSSILS

A fossil is evidence of life from the past. Fossil bones, teeth, and tracks found in the earth have taught us everything we know about dinosaurs.

LONG AND STRONG

Brachiosaurus belonged to a group of dinosaurs called sauropods. These dinosaurs had long necks and tails. They walked on four legs. Other dinosaurs in this group include Apatosaurus and Diplodocus.

strong tail

shorter hind legs

small head with tiny brain

nostrils on top of head

curved, spoonlike teeth

long neck

long front legs

Brachiosaurus had a long neck like a giraffe. But Brachiosaurus was much bigger. A Brachiosaurus weighed more than 20 giraffes!

BIG BODY, TINY HEAD

Brachiosaurus had a
tiny head compared
to its large body. Inside
its head was an even
smaller brain.

The dinosaur had two nostrils on top of its head. Long ago, scientists thought this meant Brachiosaurus lived in water. The nostril position would have allowed the dinosaur to breathe while its body was underwater. Now scientists know Brachiosaurus lived on land.

Brachiosaurus tracks were found in North America. This also shows that the dinosaur lived on land.

LONG NECK

Brachiosaurus' neck was about 40 feet (12 m) long. That's as tall as a four-story building! The dinosaur's long neck allowed it to eat leaves from plants and trees.

Though big, the dinosaur's neck was not very heavy. Brachiosaurus' backbones were hollow like a bird's bones are today. Because its bones were so light, Brachiosaurus could move its neck around like a giraffe.

In addition to sauropods, theropods such as Tyrannosaurus Rex had hollow bones.

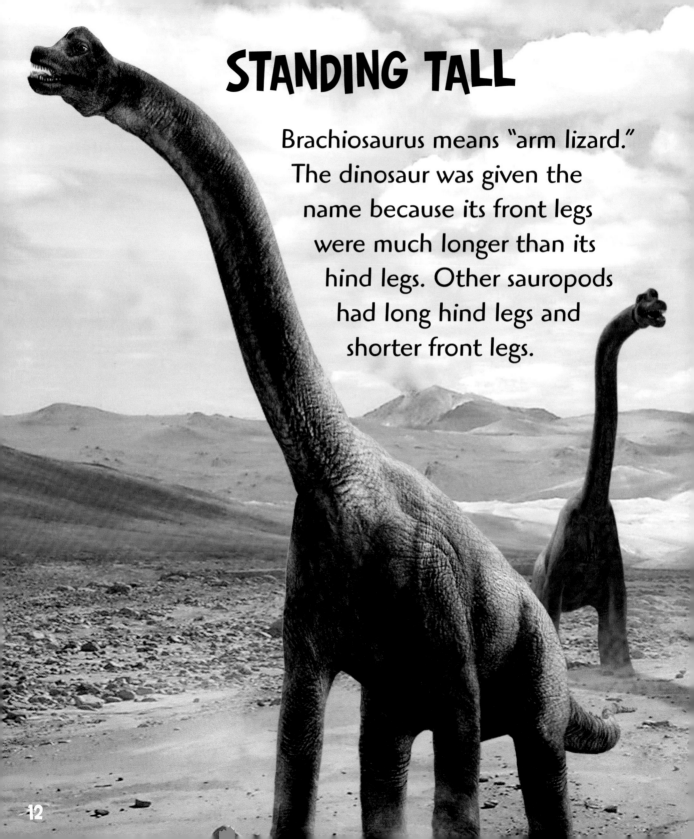

STANDING TALL

Brachiosaurus means "arm lizard."
The dinosaur was given the
name because its front legs
were much longer than its
hind legs. Other sauropods
had long hind legs and
shorter front legs.

Brachiosaurus had five toes on each foot. Padding on its feet supported the dinosaur's weight. A sharp claw stuck out from its front feet. Three back toes also had claws.

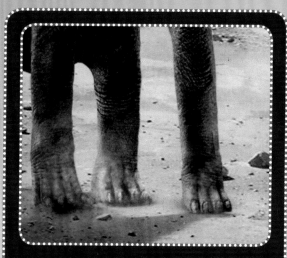

Scientists think the dinosaur's claws were used to fight off predators or collect food. Brachiosaurus could also use its claws to dig into the ground.

JURASSIC HOME

During the Jurassic Period, the earth was warm and tropical. Plants grew everywhere. Giant dinosaurs such as Camarasaurus and Diplodocus roamed.

Brachiosaurus lived in what is now western North America, in the states of Wyoming, Colorado, and Utah. It made its home in plains and forests.

Other Jurassic Animals

Apatosaurus

Allosaurus

Diplodocus

Stegosaurus

The Jurassic Period lasted from 200 million to 145 million years ago.

DINOSAUR ERA

TRIASSIC   JURASSIC   CRETACEOUS

252   200   145   66   present

millions of
years ago

DINNER TIME

Brachiosaurus was an herbivore.
This means it ate only plants.

A brachiosaurus could eat 400 pounds (180 kg) of food per day.

The dinosaur spent most of its day eating and searching for food. Its long neck allowed it to eat from the tops of trees. Young dinosaurs also ate ferns, conifers, and cycads near the ground.

Few other animals could reach the dinosaur's food.

ROCK STAR

Brachiosaurus had 56 spoonlike teeth. But its teeth weren't used for chewing. Instead, the dinosaur used them to pull leaves off trees.

Brachiosaurus swallowed its food whole. To break up the food, the dinosaur also swallowed rocks. These rocks are called gastroliths. The gastroliths rolled around in the dinosaur's stomach. They helped break down plants into a paste. This made the plants easier to digest.

Several modern birds swallow small bits of gravel and rock to help digest food.

LIVING IN HERDS

Brachiosaurus may have traveled in herds of up to 20 dinosaurs. The herds moved each day to find new food sources.

The dinosaurs tried to stay on dry, flat land as they moved. Their heavy bodies could get stuck in the muddy ground.

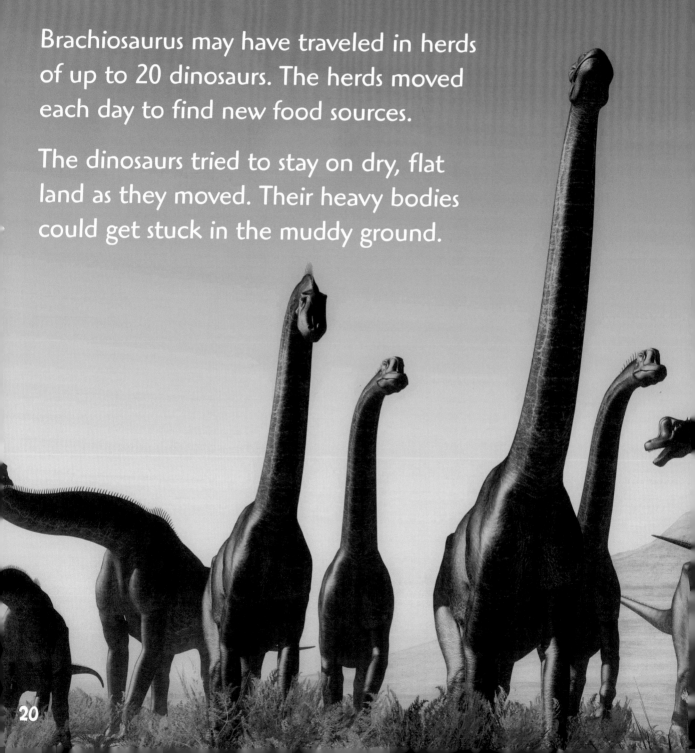

elephant herd in South Africa

Today many herbivores travel together to find food. Elephants walk up to 16 hours each day to find enough plants to eat.

STAYING SAFE

Because of its large size, Brachiosaurus had few predators. Its long tail could hit hungry meat eaters. Its thick legs could crush enemies that came too close.

Predators tried to eat young dinosaurs. To protect them, the Brachiosaurus herd may have formed a circle. The larger dinosaurs kept the smaller, younger ones safe inside the circle.

Allosaurus

One strike from Brachiosaurus' sharp claws could keep away meat-eating dinosaurs such as Allosaurus.

DINO YOUNG

Like most dinosaurs, Brachiosaurus hatched from eggs. The dinosaur's eggs were large, thick, and shaped like soccer balls. Brachiosaurus babies were only about the size of large cats when they were born.

Fossils of young sauropods are rare. In 2007 fossils from a young dinosaur were found in Wyoming. Scientists first thought it was a Diplodocus. Now scientists think it could be a Brachiosaurus.

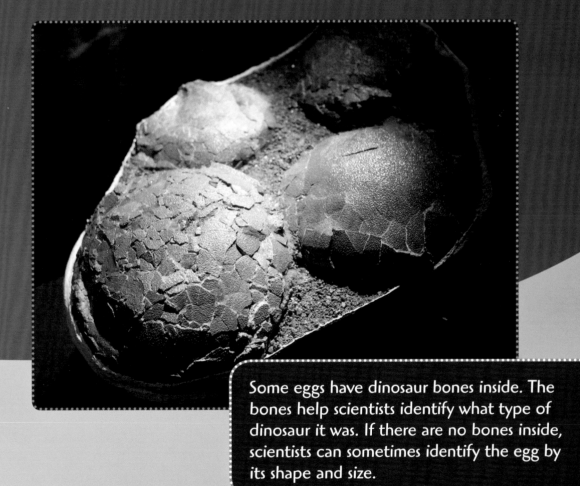

Some eggs have dinosaur bones inside. The bones help scientists identify what type of dinosaur it was. If there are no bones inside, scientists can sometimes identify the egg by its shape and size.

FINDING FOSSILS

In 1900 paleontologist Elmer Riggs found what was thought to be the first Brachiosaurus fossil in the Morrison Formation in Colorado. But Brachiosaurus was discovered much earlier. Othniel Marsh found the first Brachiosaurus fossil in 1883, but he mislabeled it as a Camarasaurus. Scientists correctly identified the fossil in 1998.

Scientists continue to uncover new information about sauropods and other dinosaurs.

"We now have to . . . re-evaluate what we thought we knew about how dinosaurs worked. . . . We need to start looking for new and different evidence."
—paleontologist Emily Rayfield

a Brachiosaurus skeleton on display in the National History Museum, Berlin, Germany

DIE WELT IM OBEREN JURA

LIGHTS, CAMERA, ACTION!

Brachiosaurus has always been a Hollywood favorite. The dinosaur has been featured in many movies, including *Jurassic Park,* *Jurassic Park III,* and *The Land Before Time.*

In *Jurassic Park,* a Brachiosaurus herd grazes among the trees. But Brachiosaurus stood on its hind legs in the movie. Most scientists agree that the real dinosaur couldn't have done this.

In *The Land Before Time,* the character Shorty was a Brachiosaurus.

Characters Alan Grant and Ellie Sattler encounter a Brachiosaurus in one of the opening scenes of *Jurassic Park*.

GLOSSARY

conifer—a tree with cones and narrow leaves called needles

cycad—a plant shaped like a tall pineapple, with a feathery crown of palmlike leaves

fern—a plant with finely divided leaves called fronds; ferns are commonly found in damp woods and on mountains

fossil—evidence of life from the geologic past

gastrolith—stomach stones used to grind up food

herd—a group of animals that lives or moves together

Jurassic Period—the second period of the Mesozoic Era; when birds first appeared

Mesozoic Era—the age of dinosaurs, which includes the Triassic, Jurassic, and Cretaceous periods; when the first birds, mammals, and flowers appeared

nostrils—openings in the nose used to breathe and smell

paleontologist—a scientist who studies fossils

predator—an animal that hunts other animals for food

sauropods—a group of closely related giant dinosaurs with long necks, thick bodies, and long tails

tropical—hot, wet, and humid

CRITICAL THINKING QUESTIONS

1. Brachiosaurus was a sauropod. Name two other dinosaurs in this group.

2. Brachiosaurus traveled in herds to find food. Name an animal today that travels in herds to find food.

3. Describe how a Brachiosaurus herd kept the smaller, younger dinosaurs safe.

READ MORE

Gregory, Josh. *Brachiosaurus*. 21st Century Junior Library: Dinosaurs. Ann Arbor, Mich.: Cherry Lake Publishing, 2016.

Rissman, Rebecca. *Brachiosaurus and Other Long-Necked Dinosaurs*. Dinosaur Fact Dig. North Mankato, Minn.: Capstone Press, 2017.

Troupe, Thomas Kingsley. *I Want to Be a Brachiosaurus*. I Want to Be ... North Mankato, Minn.: Picture Window Books, 2016.

INTERNET SITES

Use FactHound to find Internet sites related to this book.

Visit *www.facthound.com*

Just type in 9781543505429 and go.

Check out projects, games and lots more at
www.capstonekids.com

INDEX